Meet little Arnie, a cat so small and so spry,
With orange and black stripes, looked like a tiger in disguise.

HE LIVED A GOOD LIFE, AT HOME JUST THE THREE,
MOM, LEENA, DAD, MAX, IN A WARM HOUSE FILLED WITH GLEE.

But today was special, an adventure they had planned,
An outing to see animals, surely wouldn't that be grand.

THE TICKETS WERE PURCHASED,
AND SNACKS WERE IN TOW,
NOTHING COULD STOP
THEM FOR THE GRANDEST OF SHOWS.
OPEN

They got through the gates, Arnie ready to play,
But just as they'd started, Arnie got lost looking the wrong way.

He searched high and low, left and right, all around!
But his family, that he loved, was nowhere to be found...

At first, he was scared,
not sure what to do,
But he realized he could ask
for help, but who? Who?

HE CAME ACROSS A MONKEY THAT WAS SWINGING IN THE TREES,
AND ASKED HIM FOR HELP, BUT HE REPLIED, "EEE EEE, NO SIREE!"

NEXT, HE SAW A GIRAFFE
WITH ITS HEAD UP SOOOOOO HIGH, ARNIE SHOUTED
UP FOR HELP, BUT ALAS... THE GIRAFFE JUST SIGHED.

He soon saw a hippo, in a pond taking a bath,
He asked her to help find his family,
but the hippo just laughed

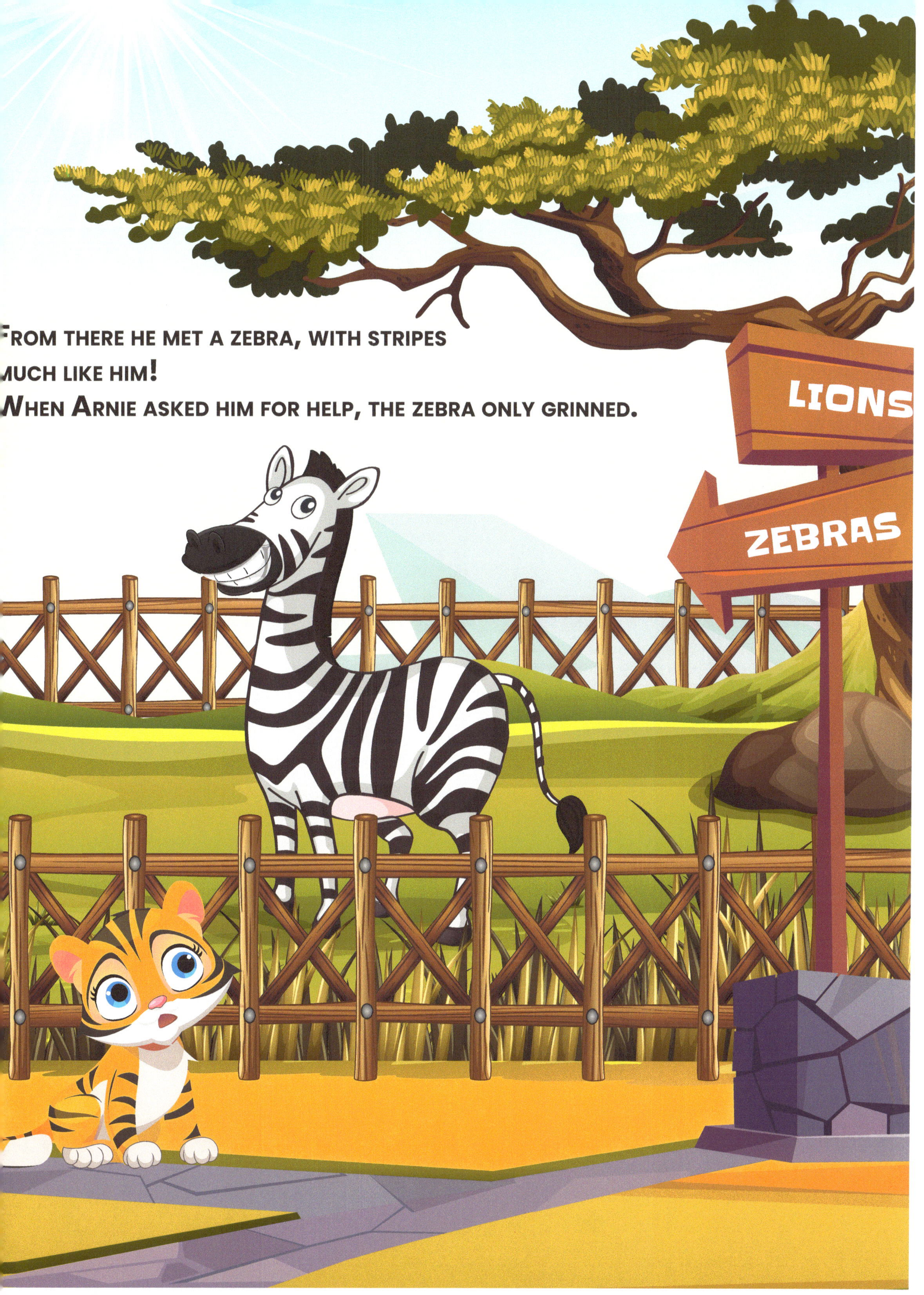

FROM THERE HE MET A ZEBRA, WITH STRIPES
MUCH LIKE HIM!
WHEN ARNIE ASKED HIM FOR HELP, THE ZEBRA ONLY GRINNED.
LIONS
ZEBRAS

AFTER THAT CAME AN ELEPHANT, SO BIG AND SO STRON
ARNIE EXCLAIMED, "HELP! MR. ELEPHANT,"
BUT THE ELEPHANT JUST YAWNED.

FINALLY, HE MET A BEAR WITH A FIERCE, SCARY SCOWL,
ARNIE CAUTIOUSLY ASKED FOR HELP, BUT THE BEAR SIMPLY GROWLED.

ARNIE HAD WALKED ALL AROUND, WITH NOTHING TO SHOW,
WHERE WAS HIS FAMILY, WHERE ELSE COULD HE GO!?
ZOO
MONKEYS
ELEPHANTS
HIPPO

Arnie was sad, scared, and walking all alone,
But then he saw a tiger, who was sitting on a throne.

THE TIGER WAS BIG, WHILE ARNIE WAS SO SMALL, HE THOUGHT,
WE'RE THE SAME... ONLY I'M SHORT AND HE'S TALL!

Arnie said to the tiger, "Are you my real family?
Perhaps we are bound?" "It must be!
We're related! Both of us with stripes all around!"

BUT THE TIGER JUMPED DOWN, "NO, WE ARE NOT THE SAME!"
"GO FIND YOUR TRUE FAMILY," HE BOLDLY EXCLAIMED.

ARNIE FELT LOW, AND NEARLY GAVE UP. BUT NOPE!
HE HAD TO KEEP SEARCHING, HE WOULDN'T
GIVE UP HOPE.

It was nearing closing time,
Arnie had to work fast,
All the animals were now sleeping,
there was no one left to ask!
ZOO
GIRAFFES
ELEPHANTS
HIPPO
LIONS
ZEBRAS
OPE

But as fate would have it, before daylight turned black,
There were Arnie's parents, overjoyed to have him back.

They hugged him so tight, and
gave him a treat, And Max said,
"We missed you so much,
now our family's complete!"

EN LEENA CHIMED IN, WITH SOME LIFE-ALTERING NEWS,
E'VE ONE MORE TO ADD, FOR A NEW BABY BREWS.

FOR A MOMENT, ARNIE JUST SAT THERE, SHOCKED AND CONFUSED, HE WAS JUST LOST, NOW HE'S GOI
TO BE A BIG BROTHER TOO?!

REUNITED TOGETHER, A TRIO PLUS ONE!
IT WAS TIME TO GO HOME, A NEW CHAPTER HAD BEGUN.